YOU'RE IT!

How to Play the Game of Life

Wisdom
for All Ages

By Ginger and Will Hannah

Illustrated by Jeanne A. Benas

Illustrations Copyright © Jeanne A. Benas
www.BenasArt.com

Edited by Liza Frenette www.lizafrenette.com
and Laura Shore www.farmsharestudio.com

Graphic/Book Design by Jen Danchetz
www.d2creativestudio.com

Cover sun photo Copyright ©
Cammeraydave/Dreamstime.com

Published by: Creative Vision Enterprises, Inc.
131 Main St., Altamont, NY 12009

ISBN Paperback: 979-8-9893463-3-2
ISBN Hardcover: 979-8-9893463-4-9

GIFTS FOR YOU!

We've created two gifts for you to best use the PLAYTAG keys! To download your free gifts, go to our website at:
www.GingerAndWillHannah.com.

PLAYTAG KEYS

PICTURE

LET GO

AFFIRM

YOU'RE IT!

TRUST

ACT

GIVE THANKS FOR THE GIFT

Create a Great Life Worksheet

**Who do you want to be?
What do you want to do?**

Dream BIG!

How Big?
There's really no limit,
if it rings true to you
and your whole heart is in it!

Time flies when you are having fun.

- Albert Einstein

YOU'RE IT!

How to Play the Game of Life

Wisdom
for All Ages

By Ginger and Will Hannah

Illustrated by Jeanne A. Benas

Let's Play Tag!

There's a child inside of you
ready to play,
who is fun and creative -

so whaddaya say?

Each letter in

P·L·A·Y·T·A·G

gives you a key
to open your mind

to all you can be

Turn every key and
you will begin to

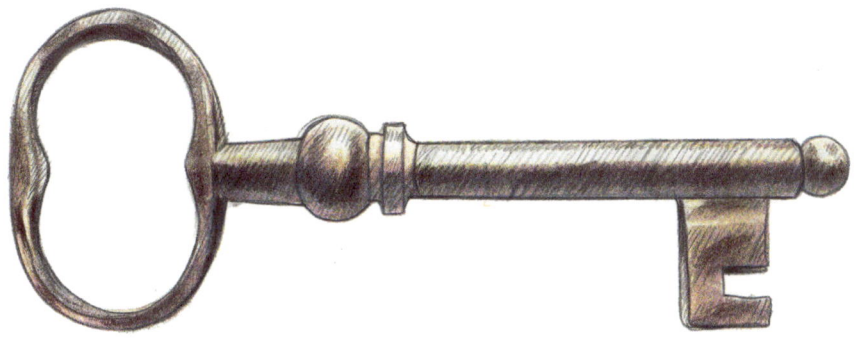

unlock the
remarkable power
within you.

P is for **Picture**

Imagine we're having a
wonderful day
chasing our dreams
with a **game** we can play!

Of all of the many things
calling to you

if you could do
anything
what would you **do**?

Life
doesn't ask you to

sit down
and wait . . .

What do you
STAND FOR
and choose
to **CREATE?**

Dream BIG!

How big?
There's really no limit,
if it rings true to you
and your whole heart is in it!

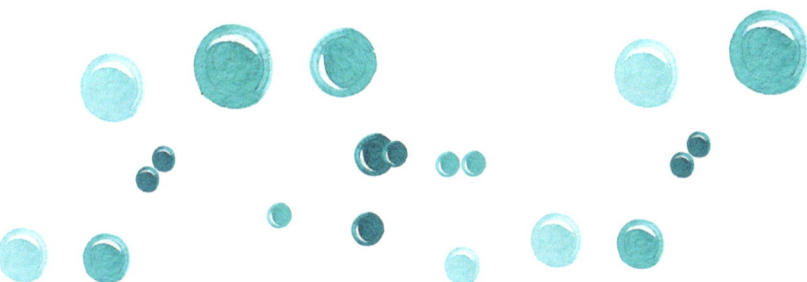

The field is wide open -
your thoughts can run free!
What bubbles up?
Tell me - **what do you SEE?**

Imagine you're happy.
Treasure the sight!
**Picture the best in you
coming to light.**

CREATE a COLLAGE

Snip it n' paste it.
Make it so real
you can practically **TASTE** it!

Feel it

Color it

Strike every chord

WAKE UP and **BEHOLD**

your new
VISION BOARD!

Good Times · **Who I am** · *My Great Idea*

What I Choose · **My Face Here** · *Happy Places*

Helping Others · **Where I am** · **This or Something Better**

Ta-Da!

...Now...

The past is  not here

The future's not yet

So open your **PRESENT** and see what you get!

TO YOU

Connect every dot
you can spot right away.

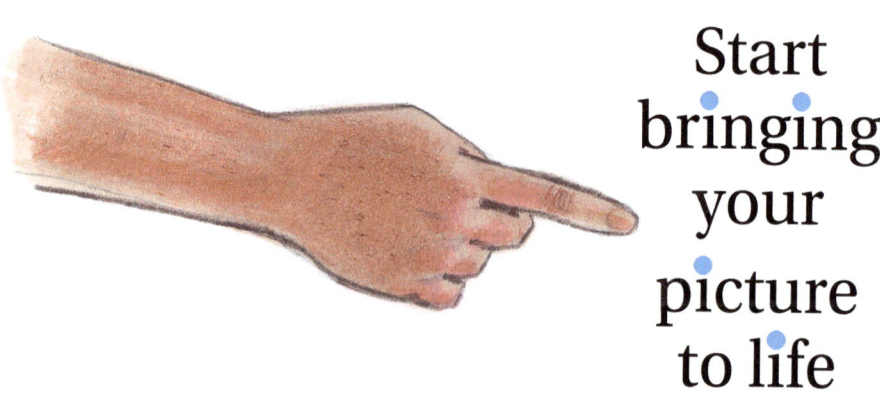

Start
bringing
your

picture
to life

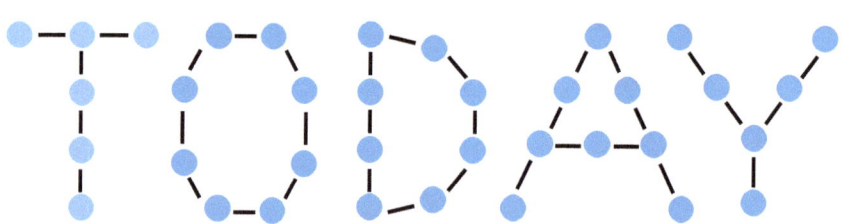

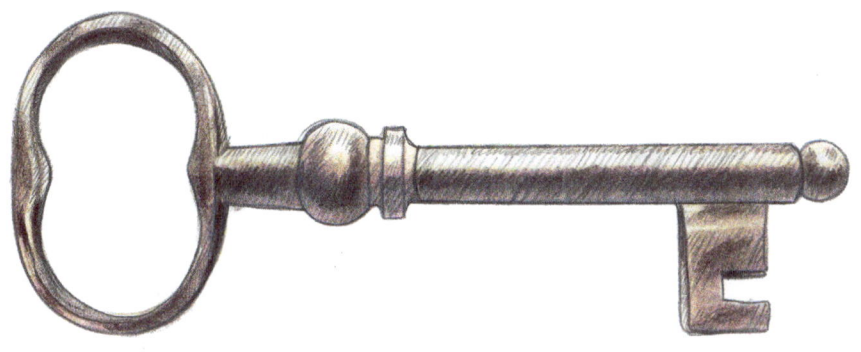

Picture
your life as a **GAME**
you can play!

L is **Let Go**

Let Go
of the thought that you
can't play right now.

Those
ROCKS
in your
backpack

are dragging you down.

But it's **easy** to

backtrack

once you know how
to turn all those rocks into

stepping stones

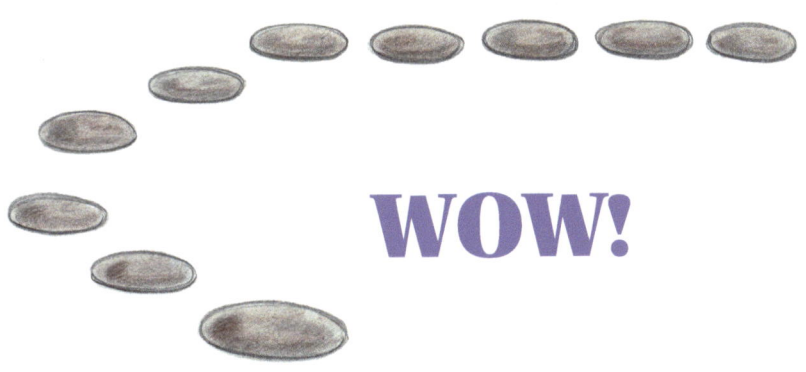

WOW!

Just Whistle ♫

Your little friend

TOTO

will come and will sit,

pinpoint the thought

and

Think **O**f **T**he **O**pposite

Sad to *Happy*
Stuck to *Free*
Afraid to *Brave*
Worried to *Whee!*

Accept where you are...
but don't stay caught.
Focus your mind on
the **POSITIVE** thought!

SO...
Tied up in knots?

Imagine a spa!

Focus on something that makes you say AHHH...

Your feelings will follow

the thoughts that you claim

and

ABRACADABRA

you're back in the game!

Make friends with your
feelings -
everyone's got 'em.

Accept every part of you -

**Top
to
Bottom.**

Whatever may
happen,
believe me -
it's true...

you're going to grow
and learn something new!

Be willing to...

Let go of judgment.
Forgive everyone -
especially **YOU!**

What's done is done.

Picture yourself with a smile
as you say...

*I'm really on top
of my game today!*

Let Go
of all doubt that can
get in your way!

A is **Affirm**

Affirmations are
POWERFUL PHRASES
that give what we picture

A Firm Foundation

You *say* what you want like it's **ALREADY SO**

I *see* myself baking

I'm rolling in dough!

Remember - words matter.
Be mindful and clear.

What you say
with commitment is
bound to appear.

I am playful,

ENTHUSIASTIC!

Confident,
friendly
and
feeling
fantastic!

Choose your **OWN** phrase - Keep it

Short n' Sweet

Make it easy to use and

Fun to repeat
Fun to repeat
Fun to repeat

I am good to myself.
I give myself credit.
I like who I am -
and that's that.
There - I said it!

Declare what you want -
the choices are endless.
State your intent
to do something

TREMENDOUS!

Say... My life is mine.
Anything's Possible!

This is my time and
I AM
UNSTOPPABLE!

SO...
Who do YOU choose to be?
Someone courageous?
Somebody kind?
Someone kind of outrageous?

Use words that **EXCITE** you
and **SHAKE** you **AWAKE.**

*I am free to be me with
each step that I take!*

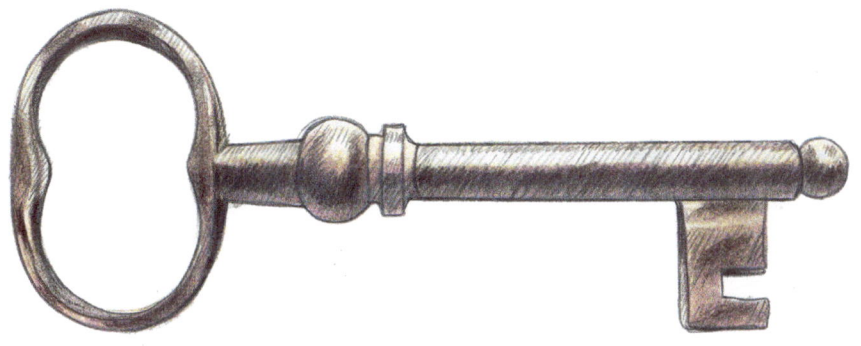

Affirm
All is Well
with each move
that you make!

Y is You're It!

Nobody else can
live your life **FOR** you,
no matter how much
they may love
and **ADORE** you.

ONLY YOU
can truly be you

and decide every day
what you're going to do.

YOU
are the one
who plays your part,
speaks your voice

and opens your heart.

And oh, what a
Beautiful Being
you are!
Have you any idea?

I don't know where to start...

IN ALL OF THE
GALAXY

Dear One - It's TRUE
No one's discovered
a MARVEL like

Who can **REASON**
and **THINK**
and **EXPLORE**
what is ours,

Swim in the ocean...

and reach for the stars!

So... NO MORE

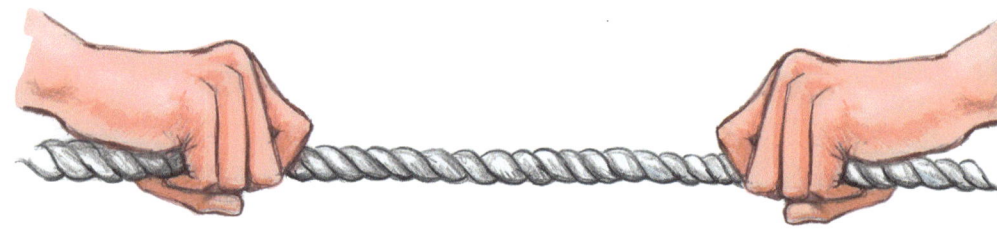

TUG OF WAR

inside of you.

DROP THE ROPE
and it's over.

Finally! Phew!

Be on your own side
in every endeavor,

and you are your very own
BEST FRIEND FOREVER!

Some people look up
and wish on a star,
but it's better to be one.
Just **BE** who you **ARE.**

SHINE!

and see what wonders await.
You are one of a kind
who can do something
GREAT!

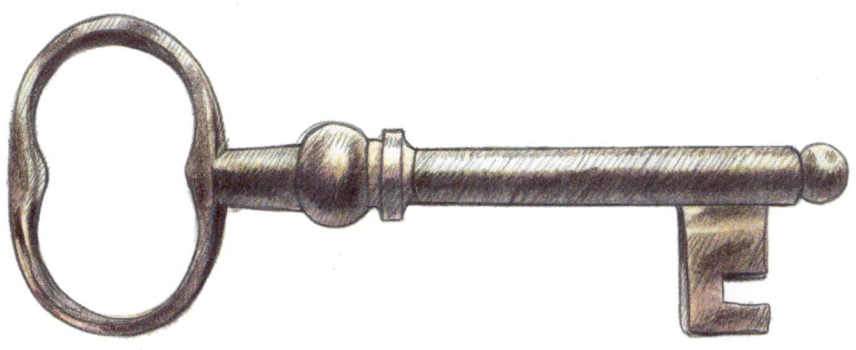

You're It!
Have fun - be happy!
CREATE!

T is for **Trust**

Trust the Universe

Think of it as your
INVISIBLE FRIEND.
It has stories to tell
and a hand to lend.

It's BIG and abundant,
It's old and it's new.

It's full of **SURPRISES.**
Guess what?
SO ARE YOU!

Trust Yourself

Go within - and begin
by calming your mind

and allowing yourself
to be caring and kind.

Be willing to learn

and you'll know what to do.
Trust that you're now on

the right path for you!

Trust Your Dreams

Each of us has our own sense of direction.

Our dreams open doors to a WHOLE NEW Dimension!

BELIEVE

that your dreams
are meant to come true.
There's a *reason*
your dreams
are **CALLING** to you!

Trust the Signs

When the Universe sends you
a Magical Sign

it sends a *Dazzling Thrill*
up your spine!

The timing is perfect.

The message is clear.

Something
AMAZING
is happening here!

Trust in Love

Day by day
we come to
discover
**we're at
our best
when we love
one another.**

You can depend on
the **power of love**
to guide and provide you
with more than enough.

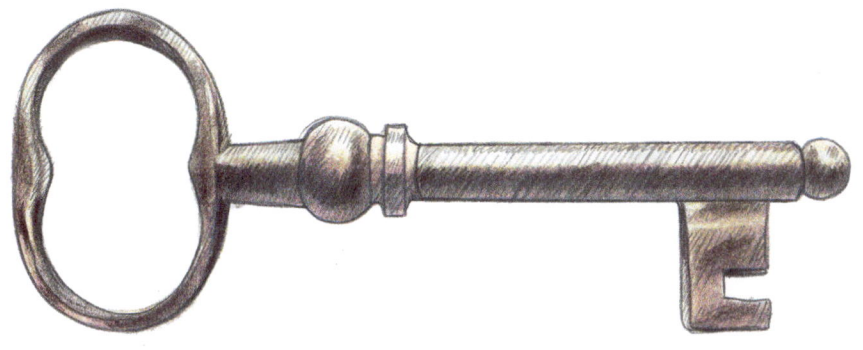

Trust
in Great Love -
it's the stuff
that you're made of!

P·L·A·Y·T·A·G

A is for Act

Act as if
you can do it already.

Imagine that!

Applause!

Confetti!

Follow your heart
and start doing it NOW.

Butterflies?
No Surprise...

You're
EXCITED!
WOW!

The name of the game
is to say

Yes I can!

Plan your Actions,
and **ACT** on your Plan.

Is your dream
to be BRAVE?

**STAND YOUR
GROUND.**

More
ACROBATIC?

Start
**BOUncing
Around!**

Take your ideas
out for a spin.

What brings you **JOY?**

What is stirring within?

It's never too early

and never too late

to open your mind
and begin to **CREATE!**

Take **small daily steps** -

that's all there is to it.

And make a

BIG LEAP

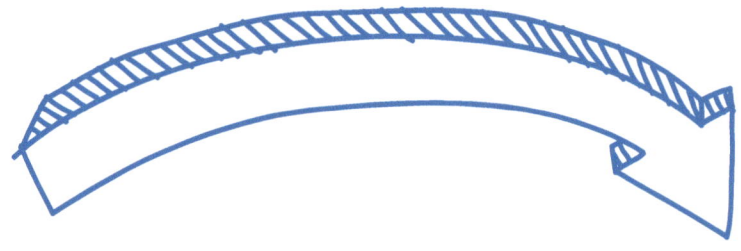

when you're ready to **DO IT!**

Rise up and **sing.**
Do what you love!

Start **LIVING** the life
you've been **dreaming** of!

Keep this in mind -
every wise person knows
what we look for we find.
What we focus on **GROWS.**

SO... Look for the good.
Celebrate Love!
Step up and show us
the stuff that you're made of!

Act
like there's nothing
that you
are afraid of.

P·L·A·Y·T·A·G

G is **Give Thanks**
For You

Give
yourself
kudos for
taking a
chance

for playing your
heart out and

DANCING the dance.

You choose to be happy -
you laugh out loud.

You believe in the best -
and expect to be
WOWED!

Give Thanks

For Friends and Family

Appreciate those
who encourage and guide you.

Root for them all
as they run alongside you!

Say...
Thank you for loving me -
I love you too!

It's so good to say,
and so easy to do.

Give Thanks
For Peace and Quiet

(Try it)

Here's a time-honored tip:

However life goes,
the answer is always
right under your nose.

Stop...

Smell the roses

Breathe in - nice n' slow

Now blow out the candles

and let it all go...

Give Thanks

For Freedom

Live in the moment.
Enjoy what you do!

When you let go of worries,
they let go of **YOU.**

Negative thoughts?
None of us need 'em.

Choose inner peace -
it's your pathway to
FREEDOM.

Give Thanks
For Wisdom

The love of the game is
discovering **YOU!**

Now let others know
they are wonderful too.

Play Tag is for everyone!
Pass it on - HEY!

Let's **ALL** have
the time of our lives today.

Give Thanks
for these keys
as you happily say:

Picture your life
as a game you can play.

Let Go of all doubt
that can get in your way.

Affirm all is well with each
move that you make.

You're It!
Have fun - be happy! Create!

Trust in great love - it's the
stuff that you're made of.

Act like there's nothing
that you are afraid of.

Give Thanks for these keys
as you happily say:

TAG! YOU'RE IT!
Hip Hip Hooray!

Watching you play is
SUCH FUN

It's **STUNNING!**

GREAT GAME!

YOU'VE GOT THIS!

GIVE THANKS FOR THE GIFT! ▶ PICTURE ▶ LET GO ▶ AFFIRM ▶ YOU'RE IT ▶ TRUST ▶ ACT ▶

**YOU'RE OFF
AND RUNNING!**

SHARE YOUR STORIES / CREATIONS!

Imagine you're happy.
Treasure the sight!
**Picture the best in you
coming to light.**

As you use ALL the PLAYTAG keys together, you will begin to create your heart's desires! Those could be:

- Traits you develop, like confidence and courage
- Having fun adventures and making new friends
- New skills you learn

Whatever they are, we'd love to hear about them! Share your stories and creations on our website: www.GingerAndWillHannah.com.

THANK YOU FOR READING OUR BOOK!

We hope you enjoyed it and are excited about using the PLAYTAG keys to create a great life!

We would appreciate your feedback and look forward to reading what you have to say.

Please take two minutes now to leave us a helpful review on Amazon letting us know what you thought of the book. www.GingerAndWillHannah.com/review

As it says in our book,

Play Tag is for everyone!
Pass it on - HEY!

Let's **ALL** have
the time of our lives today!

Share these keys with your family and friends so that they have the keys to play the game of life, too!

Volume discounts are available.